Spider in a glider

Lesley Sims

Illustrated by David Semple

Spider is spinning her sparkling strings.

Swaying from branches,
she sings as she swings.

"I wish to fly

so I'm making some wings!"

She creeps
up a rock

and then leaps
into space.

What a shock! With a splat,
she lands flat on her face.

"I'll try it again.
I will fly!" declares Spider.

She falls even harder,
but Beetle has spied her.

"I can't fly either,"
sighs Beetle, beside her,
"though I tried and I tried.

So... I built my own glider!"

The glider is gleaming
and ready to ride.

Beetle and Spider
both clamber inside.

Dragonfly tows them up...

...high in the sky.

Then Beetle
lets go...

They glide in
wide circles

and ride on
the breeze.

The wind blows below them...

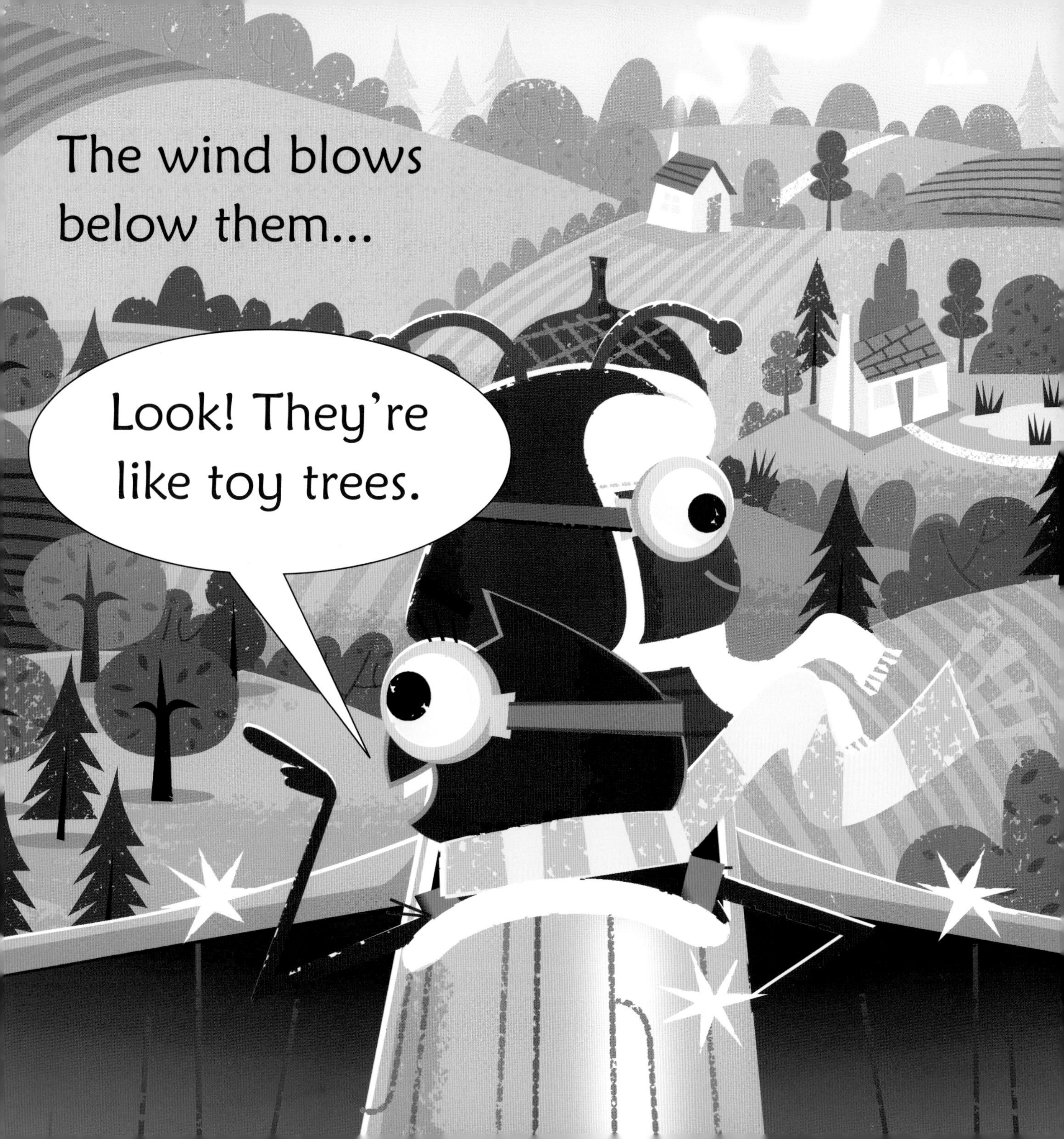

The wind starts to huff and to puff.
Thunder booms.

With a crack and a spark,
a bright lightning strike looms.

The glider is tossed up and down
and around.

"All is lost!" Beetle splutters.
"We'll crash to the ground."

But Spider starts spinning.
Her legs are a blur.

"I'll save us!" she says,
with a *whizzz* and a *whirrr*.

They parachute down.

Now both have decided
life's best on the ground.

About phonics

Phonics is a method of teaching reading which is used extensively in today's schools. At its heart is an emphasis on identifying the *sounds* of letters, or combinations of letters, that are then put together to make words. These sounds are known as phonemes.

Starting to read
Learning to read is an important milestone for any child. The process can begin well before children start to learn letters and put them together to read words. The sooner children can discover books and enjoy stories and language, the better they will be prepared for reading themselves, first with the help of an adult and then independently.

You can find out more about phonics on the Usborne Very First Reading website, **www.usborne.com/veryfirstreading** (US readers go to **www.veryfirstreading.com**). Click on the **Parents** tab at the top of the page, then scroll down and click on **About synthetic phonics**.

Phonemic awareness

An important early stage in pre-reading and early reading is developing phonemic awareness: that is, listening out for the sounds within words. Rhymes, rhyming stories and alliteration are excellent ways of encouraging phonemic awareness.

In this story, your child will soon identify the long *i* sound, made by the *i-e* combination, as in **wi̱de̱** and **besi̱de̱**. Look out, too, for rhymes such as **space** – **face** and **booms** – **looms**.

Hearing your child read

If your child is reading a story to you, don't rush to correct mistakes, but be ready to prompt or guide if he or she is struggling. Above all, do give plenty of praise and encouragement.

Edited by Jenny Tyler
Designed by Sam Whibley

Reading consultants: Alison Kelly and Anne Washtell

First published in 2018 by Usborne Publishing Ltd., Usborne House, 83-85 Saffron Hill, London EC1N 8RT, England.
www.usborne.com Copyright © 2018 Usborne Publishing Ltd.